Come Lord Jesus Be Our Guest

Inspirational Poems and Prayers

by

Bob Haar

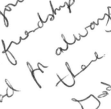

authorHOUSE™

1663 LIBERTY DRIVE, SUITE 200
BLOOMINGTON, INDIANA 47403
(800) 839-8640
WWW.AUTHORHOUSE.COM

First published by AuthorHouse 12/16/04

ISBN: 1-4208-0409-X (sc)
ISBN: 1-4208-0408-1 (dj)

Printed in the United States of America
Bloomington, Indiana

This book is printed on acid-free paper.

Table of Contents

𝕿

𝖀

𝖁

The following poems were written as part of a workshop on writing poetry as an element of the grieving process. The class was held a few months after the death of my father in January 1999.

The Storm

A snowstorm kept me from you.
The roads were closed—
No way to get there
To be with you.
You know I loved you,
Yet I wanted to tell you
Just one more time.
The uncooperative snow, however,
Buried my grief
And it's still snowing.

Bob Haar

The Hand

I would gently stroke your forehead,
Feel the cold smoothness of your skin.
I would not wish you back,
But my hand longs to touch
The icy evenness of your forehead…
One last time.

The Cold

Why is death in January
So much colder than even the most frigid winter?

Bob Haar

Distant Horizon

There is a distant horizon
That beckons me; calls out to me
I follow its summons,
But the path is muddy and slow.
Downed tree limbs impede my progress.
I crawl over them slowly
Rivers cover their banks,
So I tread water, deliberately, carefully
The final ascent is steep,
So I climb it languidly.
Reaching the summit, I see the horizon again.
The sun is shining brightly;
There is color and warmth again.
So I travel on,
I travel on.

I Forgive You.

I forgive you
For wanting to die,
For wanting the suffering to end.
I know you wanted to stay with me longer,
But the pain was too much, too long, too great.
I forgive you.

I Can't Say

I can't say
I know how you feel
Because I don't,
I can only pray with you,
Offer you a meal or stay with you.
You know I'm here for you…you know.

Precious

Precious loved ones
Let me protect you
Like a lion guards his den
No harm shall come to you
I shall keep vigil over you
While you sleep in silence.

Bob Haar

The Void

You are gone now
I cared for you,
Held your hand in mine when you cried out for death.
I waited with you.
Together we ached till the final moment arrived.
Now you are home,
But I still remember your calls for suffering's end.
The void tears me apart.
You are gone now.

The following poems were written for a college creative writing class in the 1970s.

Lonely Prayer

My dearest savior, my legs were not broken,
But at times I feel my side has been pierced
By spears of a life that was spoken
Rather than acted upon.
I could not bear to equal your sorrow.
My dreams of today and tomorrow
Are realized in my mind, not in my life
Your goal was to die and live again
While mine is just to live.
Give me a purpose; give me strife
To overcome and conquer.
Grant me a warning hand
To soothe my bloodied palms.
Give me other lives to pray for,
Not just my own.

Bob Haar

The Revolving Door

It starts with a lump—
And a thousand worries—
Praying against malignancy.
We choke back our tears
As the advent of chemotherapy
Confirms our fears.
She complains to God, but never to us,
As the automatic hospital door
Becomes revolving.
We sit and talk about grandchildren
And it ends with hope,
Where life exists…

The Power of the Bended Knee

When troubles soar and fortunes wane,
We've much to lose but naught to gain.
When feelings reach their lowest yet,
We mustn't quit; we mustn't fret.
We all should rise to bended knee,
Where tears are poured on Calvary.
There we shall find our resting place,
Sweet refuge in our savior's face.

Refuge: Number One

Father, my life is empty without you.
Hymns and prayers about you
Prove lifeless on my lips.
My soul is a desert
Yearning for salt that will make it thirsty.
Rising suns only bring hopelessness
And star-filled skies echo my sorrow and pain.
From this desolate valley,
I cannot even dream
Of viewing the mere foot of your glorious mountain.
Help me, Father.
This climb will take strong hands and feet,
But it will take an even stronger heart.
Give my weakened organ to your son
And sharing each other's sorrow,
Together we will conquer valleys, mountains.
My soul's desert will then become an oasis
Of living water.

Easter Portrait

Head bowed from the pain of a crown of thorns,
Blood and salty tears roll down His cheeks
And moisten His tangled beard. Arms outstretched,
Wrists tied to the wood.
Hands weak,
palms like posters nailed to trees—
Spiked to the cross
Slender chest reddened by the sun—muddied from the multitude.
Bloated stomach—loose cloth cinched 'round bony hips
And bruised thighs.
Knees bent then straightened
As curling toes reach for the angled platform.
Two faceless men who suffer with Him
Writhe off to either side
While dark clouds converge behind Him.
"It is finished."

The following poems were written to conclude sermons I have presented in 2003 and 2004.

There Is A Church

There stands a church proud on the hill
Where Christians sing and pray.
One day a storm came bursting through,
And the church was blown away.

Hymnbooks were torn
And scattered about,
The pews were splintered
The future—in doubt.

Bulldozers came and leveled the land,
Leaving nothing behind but gravel and sand.

When Sunday arrived, a miracle grew.
No hymnbooks were needed,
nor a comfortable pew.

The members they stood
And sang from the heart.
Prayers of thanksgiving
Were heard from the start.

You see this proud church
Is more than a steeple.
It's made up of friends,
Of Jesus' own people.

Signs

Can you see the signs of Christmas around:
The lights on the tree, the snow on the ground;
The church so festive with ribbons and bows;
The smell of pine trees that tickles the nose?

Wise men traveled by day and by night;
The star in the east shone so bright.
Shepherds waited for news of the birth;
Angels proclaimed good will, peace on earth.

So as we gather to remember the child,
His humble beginnings, so meek and so mild,
Let's also prepare for the future so bright,
When Jesus returns in glory and might.

Two Fish and Five Loaves of Bread

There, on the hillside, close to the beach,
It's Jesus the prophet; well within reach.

Have you seen what he's done,
The miracles and such?
Perhaps he can heal us
With simply a touch.

But the hour is late;
So hungry we are,
There are thousands to feed
And the town is so far.

A little boy cries,
"I have food; I can share"
Then Jesus looked out,
Saw the boy standing there.

"What do you have?" a disciple said.
"I have two fish and five loaves of bread."

The disciple then scoffed
At the boy's humble feast.
And the people, they grumbled
Like an impatient beast.

But Jesus looked out
At the hungering masses:
"Have them sit down,
While the evening sun passes."

Then Jesus gave thanks
For the small feast before them.
He started to share;
The meal became more then.

Everyone ate; not a one was left out,
Seeing this miracle, the people did shout.

"Our king," they cried out but then Jesus fled.
It was only two fish and five loaves of bread.

So when a miracle we see now,
Let us give thanks 'stead of asking how.

The Miracle of Lazarus

Lord, I have heard from Bethany's gate
That Lazarus is ill, so please don't wait.
Your presence is needed, so please try to hurry.
You know how Martha is given to worry.

But Jesus, He waited and waited to leave
He knew that the sisters would have to believe…
That miracles happen to all who have faith,
That hope and love can overcome hate.

Jesus arrived, went straight to the tomb.
He prayed to His Father and called to the room.
"Lazarus, come out and live life anew.
Take off your cloths and bandages too."

And so we remember that life is brief
For those whom we lose to death and grief.
Just believe in Christ: there is no doubt
That Lazarus really did come out.
Amen.

Too Busy

Our Lord Jesus was walking one everyday morn
When ten men approached him—
sad and forlorn.

A disease had claimed them;
They were frightened and lonely.
Their last hope was Jesus
So they begged him—"If only
You could free us
From Leprosy's shame
We'd give you our thanks
And honor your name."

So Jesus, He cleansed them
From Leprosy's burn,
But nine were too busy;
Only one would return.

Bob Haar

Second Chance

God forgives us, all our sin,
So let that second chance begin.
Do not hold that guilt and pain;
Let the Lord send cleansing rain.

Let His love begin to pour
And soon the shame will be no more.
If you repent, His love will bring
Redemption and your heart will sing.

Dwelling Among Us

In the beginning was the word…
Jesus, whom I know you've heard
Dwelt among us to be sure
The son of man, and yet so pure.

Spotless Lamb of God was He,
Suffered death on Calvary.
Sent to earth from God above,
So full of grace; so full of love.

Now he lives within our hearts.
Our fear of life and death depart.
He's always there—one prayer away
So won't you let him come and stay?

Bob Haar

Confession of St. Peter

Let us be like Simon Peter
When he answered Jesus' call.
"You are the true Messiah
I pledge to you my all."
Peter's faith was strong and true,
Almost unwavering to the end.
But Peter's faith, it faltered
When the rooster crowed again.
A special lesson can be learned
From Peter's loyal mission.
After all, he was a human too,
He just made a bad decision.
So let us stand together,
Proclaiming Jesus' love,
Recalling Peter's words of faith
As we confess above.

Love Is...

Love is holding your hand in prayer.
Love is knowing that God is there.
Love is listening in silent night.
Love is basking in His holy light.
Love is enduring and never ends.
Love is the spirit our Father sends.
Love never rejoices in wrongful living.
Love is ever hopeful, and oh so forgiving.
Love is the body and blood of our Lord
Love is the truth in His holy word.
Love, faith and hope reign from God above
But the greatest of these you know is love.

Roll Up Your Sleeves

The church has need of women and men
To share ensure Jesus' ministry never ceases.
Who then will answer our savior's call?
Who will say "yes" as commitment decreases?

We live in a world of comfort and ease.
Are we not challenged by God's call to service?
Just hit the snooze button, roll over again.
All this talk of God, does it make you nervous?

Now is the time to make a clear stand,
To roll up our sleeves and pitch in with joy.
Our Redeemer wants our hearts and hands
In the simplest ways, like a girl or a boy.

Jesus loves me, this is something I know.
The faith of a child can show us the way.
Will we rise from our beds and join the throng?
The answer is "yes," I hope and I pray.

Are We Ready?

Are we ready to be sent?
To show the world what God has meant
To us whose lives were changed from loss
By Jesus' pain upon the cross?

Are we ready to be gathered
As Christ's disciples, or would we rather
Just sit in a rudderless boat
Adrift in apathy – afloat?

Are we ready to be claimed
To be chosen – renamed
As instruments of Jesus' love?
Claimed, gathered, and sent,
That's really what we're made of.

Bob Haar

Let us Pray

O Lord we thank you for this day
And so we bow our heads and pray.
Instill within our hearts the zeal
To share your love, and how we feel.

We know your Spirit dwells inside
This blessed church – we cannot hide
The grace that overcomes our sin
And saves each one who enters in. Amen.

The Crown of Jesus

A tiny babe lay sleeping still.
Three kings emerged beyond the hill.
Gifts they bring to mark his birth.
A royal child to save the earth.

For 30 years he worked with wood.
A mother's son who understood
That a crown would rest upon his head,
But one of sharpened thorns instead.

As Mary looked at Jesus now
And the crown that rested on his brow,
Although the thorn was sharp and cruel.
It would become a savior's jewel.

So when we look at sparkling rings
Bracelets, necklaces, and things.
A brilliant crown – majestic, bright.
Let us think of Jesus' holy light.

Welcome Home

For years and years I've been away
I don't deserve a gala feast.
But still you welcomed home your son
The one you though had been deceased.

My brother stayed to work the land
His loyalty deserves this meal.
But still you welcomed home your son.
I can't express the shame I feel.

I lived a life of sin and lust.
Half your fortune thrown away.
But still you welcomed home your son.
The shame I feel I cannot say.

Forgive me for these sins of mine
I don't deserve your love so true.
But still you welcomed home your son.
With these kindest words: "I forgive you."

One Thief

Two thieves were crucified in Jesus' sight -
One on his left, and one on his right.
One thief wanted to be set free.
The other asked Jesus: Remember me."

One thief wanted the Messiah to act.
The other knew forgiveness was what he lacked.
One thief moaned his final fate.
One thief asked for heaven's gate.

One thief cried aloud in pain
One thief entered Christ's domain.
One thief died a lonely sinner.
One thief lived a forgiven winner.

Which thief are we, as time goes on?
Do we seek salvation when the moment's gone?
Or do we live with Jesus Christ each day?
Invite him in our hearts to stay?

I pray as time does pass us by
That faith will be our swift reply.
Forgiveness rests in Jesus' face,
Which fills the world with love and grace.

Bob Haar

Guidance

Lord God we ask for your guidance
As we prepare for this season of Lent.
We thank you and praise you Father
For the symbol of love that you sent.

Your son suffered death and betrayal
Endured pain, agony for us all.
We're so grateful for Jesus' commitment.
In humility, on our knees we must fall.

As ambassadors, help us to love you,
And as disciples help us to share
Your glorious Good News with others
And in our hearts, please live with us there.

A Simple Meal

Is it merely bread and wine?
Or does another meaning come to mind?
Jesus' precious blood was shed
So much more than just wine and bread.

He came to earth to die for sin
Through the gates of heaven, we can enter in.
Eternal life is ours to keep
Because our Savior's wounds were deep.

So as you take the wine and bread
Remember how we're truly fed.
God's love is shown through Jesus Christ,
And the body and blood thus sacrificed.

Empty

Three women came on Easter morn
With spices that they used to adorn
The body of Jesus, their fallen Lord,
But the path somehow was already worn.

They reached the tomb, and in their sight
Was an angel dressed in glowing white.
They hid their eyes from the blinding light
And wondered why the tomb was bright.

To calm their fears, the angel said:
"Why do you seek the living among the dead?
Your Lord has risen from his bed.
Come see the place where he laid his head."

The women looked – to their surprise
They hardly could believe their eyes.
Their Savior truly did arise.
Joy and wonder replaced their cries.

They ran to tell John, and Peter, too.
On the wings of love and faith, they flew.
Jesus did arise; it's true.
He overcame sin and death for you.

See the Evidence

Thomas was a doubter true
Until he saw where the nails went through.
He bowed before his risen Christ,
And remembered what he sacrificed.

Today we reaffirm our love
For God who sees us from above.
He seeks our service everyday
And so we bow our heads and pray.

Lord give us strength to share your life
With souls that suffer through pain and strife.
And may our faith be so affirmed,
That life in you is thus confirmed.

Ride On Jesus, Ride On

He came to town a humble man
Riding slowly on a colt of white.
The people thought the Messiah had come
To rid them of their imprisoned plight.

They threw their cloaks in Jesus' path.
They spread palm branches in his way.
They shouted: "holy, holy, holy!
Our freedom comes to us this day."

But Jesus freed us all from death.
The shackles of sin were thus removed.
He enters our hearts with peace and grace.
The cross is how his love was proved.

So cheer our Lord with service true
And think of others' needs and cares.
It surely is the thing to do.
To cheer our love with palms and prayers.

My Heart

Mom, you give the best of care
To all your children everywhere.
You give us food and clothing too.
We're thankful for the things you do.
We want to give you oh so much
In thanks for such a gentle touch.
For all the love that you impart
We give to you our grateful heart.

Absolution

Lord God, we humbly ask for the absolution of our sins, that you would wipe our slates clean with the body and blood of your dear son Jesus Christ. Help us to begin life anew, empowered by your Holy Spirit and dedicated in the service of others. In His name we pray. Amen

Abusive Relationship

Our Heavenly Father, we pray for help and understanding. We know that life can be frustrating and disappointing, but physical abuse is not the answer to that frustration and disappointment. Give (name) the power to seek you out and to the courage to turn from his / her violent ways. Help him / her to be mindful of his / her destructive behavior and the serious consequences that result from it. Please give him / her a peaceful heart. In Jesus' name we pray. Amen.

Accidental Death

Father, Giver of all things good and holy, we pray that you would comfort the family of _____. We don't know why you took him / her from us. All we know is that he / she is with you now, and that your love and goodness live on forever. Comfort the loved ones who are left on this earth, and evoke the feeling of joy in their hearts when they realize that some day they will be reunited with _____. In praise we ask for this. Amen.

Addiction

Lord, we search our souls for logic and reason. We know not why destructive and addictive behavior invades our minds and bodies. All we know is that we cannot end this misery alone. We need the help of you, O Father, and the friends of fellowship and compassion, to help us overcome this demon. Through your power alone, and with the help of others in recovery, we can see a new light shining down upon us. Help us to walk with you one day and one step at a time. In His name we pray. Amen.

Advent

Lord Jesus, it is the season of Advent, and we wait your coming once again. We await again for the birth of a savior, Christ the Lord, whose birth was foretold in the prophecies of old. It is a season to reflect upon life, and what it would be without the birth of that babe in Bethlehem. We cannot fathom an earth without the love of Jesus in it. Your birth gives us hope for today and tomorrow.

During this celebration of your second coming, we thank you for you love, your suffering, your death and your resurrection, which shows us the way to eternal life. In your name we pray. Amen.

AIDS Patient

Merciful Father, please be with _____, who is suffering with every breath and movement he / she takes. We dare not ask why he / she has been asked to bear such pain and agony; we simply ask that you comfort him / her and his / her family during this period of tribulation. Bring your peace and love to his / her bedside. Show him / her that death is a part of life, and soon he / she will be with you, enjoying the peace and comfort of eternal life with you. Ease his / her pain now and completely. We humbly ask this in Jesus' name. Amen.

Alzheimer's Patient

O Wonderful Counselor, we ask for your presence in the life of _____. We ask that you would restore the images he / she holds dear in his / her heart. Enable his / her heart to see and recognize his / her family once again. Enable his / her soul to witness the love and power of Your Holy Spirit. Enable his / her spirit to recognize the powerful love that completely surrounds him / her. We reach out our hands and our hearts to him / her. Help him / her to grasp them tightly, until you call him / her to his / her greater reward in heaven. All these things we ask in the name of the One who saves us daily with His death and resurrection. Amen.

Anniversary

Our Friend and Savior who was present at the wedding in Canaan to help celebrate the union of two loved ones, we ask you to bless yet another union. We thank you for the marriage of _____, and we bless you for the _____ years that have kept them together in your love. We ask that you would continue to bless them with health, happiness and abounding love. In Jesus' name we pray. Amen.

Ascension

Our Lord who lived with us on this earth, we ask that you would remember the ones you have left behind. We long to follow you up to heaven, but we know we must stay here to do your will, to minister to your children. Your ascension has given us the hope and promise of eternal life, and we wait anxiously for the day when we will join you in eternity. We thank you for this promise, and in your name we pray. Amen.

Answered Prayer

Father, we thank you for the wondrous miracle of answered prayer. You do not realize the gratitude we hold in our hearts for you. You have taken our requests and granted them because you love us, and we thank you for that abundant love and mercy.

We lift our souls up to you and give you thanks for watching over us. We express our deepest gratitude to you for taking care of our every need. We pray this in humility and in Jesus' name. Amen.

Athletic Contest

Dear Lord, we thank you for the strength and athletic abilities you have given these young men and women. Always grant them the will and desire to display their talents and do their very best. Keep them safe from harm and injury. Today and every day, we ask that the spirit of sportsmanship be ever-present. All these things we request in the name of Jesus. Amen.

ℬ

Baby

Dear Father, Our God, we come before you with grateful hearts for this new life you have granted us. Because you love us, you created us in your own image. We thank you for this new life you have bestowed upon us. Keep him / her healthy and happy throughout his / her years on this earth. As he / she matures, help him / her to grow in faith and to trust in you, the Creator. In your holy name we pray. Amen.

Banquet

Our Father in heaven, we thank you for our daily bread, and we express profound gratitude for the hands that have prepared it. Bless this food to our bodies. May it strengthen and preserve us, and may it nourish our spirits as well as our bodies. In Jesus' name we pray. Amen.

Baptism—Infant

Dearest Lord, we thank you for the life of _____. We praise you for the living water that your son, Jesus, has given to us. We ask that you would stand beside _____, as he / she grows in your love and care. Be with his / her parent(s), and give them strength to help _____ grow in faith and understanding of your word and will. In Jesus' glorious name we pray. Amen.

Baptism—Adult

Father God, Giver of all life and breath, we thank you for ____ _____. When John baptized Jesus, you said that you were well pleased. Show us your pleasure, and bless the baptism of _____ ____. Help him / her to seek your will, and to always be obedient to your commandments. May his / her faith grow and be fruitful. We ask these things in the name of your son, Jesus Christ. Amen.

Benediction

Lord God, we ask for your blessing, for your love, for your understanding, for your faithfulness and for your forgiveness, in the name of the Father, and of the Son and of the Holy Spirit. Amen.

Body of Christ

Gracious heavenly Father, as your children, we are members of the body of Christ, and we thank you for the blessings you give to us daily. Keep our fellowship strong in faith, for as the fellowship is strengthened, so too is the body nourished and sustained. And to those who are separated from our fellowship, we ask that you would give them the desire and strength to return to us so that they too might partake of this spiritual camaraderie. In your holy name we pray. Amen.

Boss / Supervisor / Manager

Dear Jesus, you know above anyone else the sacrifice that is required for leadership. In our workplace, that leadership is tested on a daily basis. We humbly ask that you would strengthen our managers and supervisors. Give them wisdom and compassion to lead in ways that instruct and inspire all of us. Guide them down a straightforward and honest pathway, as you have led us and continue to lead us. Give us the power to put forth the best that we have for our leaders on a consistent daily basis. Help our work to always be fruitful and honorable. In your name we pray. Amen.

Bread of Life

Our Father, Giver of all that is good and holy, we thank and praise you for your son, Jesus. Help us always to remember that he was and is the bread of life. Nourish us daily with that bread. Strengthen us with that spiritual food that sustains us through trouble and heartache. Instill within us a deep hunger for that bread, always studying your word and seeking out your will. In your son, the bread of life's name, we pray. Amen.

Bride

Lord Jesus, we ask for your blessing on _____ as she marries _____ today. Give her the strength to be a trusting

and patient wife. Let her joy be complete as she becomes one with
_____. We pray for her complete happiness, and ask that
you would guide this marriage with your loving hand. In your name
we pray. Amen.

Brother

Dear Lord, please be with my brother. You know the hard times
he is experiencing these days. Please strengthen him in the coming
days so that he might meet these challenges head on. Give him
courage and trust, and the realization that you are with him always,
even into the end of the age. In Jesus' name I pray. Amen.

Building Dedication

Our Gracious Father, Builder and Creator of the world we live
in, we ask for your blessing on this new facility. May it serve as an
inspiration to your servants. May it become an instrument of your
ministry to be used to your glory and as a witness to those who seek
your Word and truth. We thank you for the hands that have laid each
brick, and we express gratitude for all those who have contributed to
its completion. We dedicate this structure to the One who has saved
us all. In God, the creator's name, we pray. Amen.

Burden

Holy God, I ask for your help and salvation. I humbly request
that the burden that has consumed my life be lifted. Grant me release
from the pain and suffering of everyday life. Strengthen me so that
I may do your service and bid your will. And give me continued

courage to seek you out when I become weak and overburdened. I ask this in your son's name. Amen.

<u>Burn Victim</u>

Our Gracious Lord in heaven, we ask for your blessing on ___ _____. We do not know why he / she has to suffer with these wounds of fire, but we do know that you are with him / her in his / her hour of need. Comfort and protect him / her from further agony and pain, and let your healing hands touch our wounded friend. Let your hands bring soothing serenity. Be with the doctors and nurses who minister to burn victims. Give them strength and compassion as they minister to their patients. All these things we ask in the name of Jesus. Amen.

<u>Business</u>

Lord Jesus, we ask for the continued success of _____. May the services and products we offer be of service to you and your people. Give all of our employees a sense of duty and dedication so that in serving us they might also serve you.

Help us always to be truthful and honest with our customers, and, if it be your will, grant us a successful year in all that we do. In your name we pray. Amen.

C

Cancer Patient

Lord, we simply ask that you would be with _____, who is suffering from the dreaded disease of cancer. Give him / her strength as he / she battles on and on, not knowing when the end of the suffering might come. Grant him / her pardon and release him / her from the pain that burdens his / her life. Be with the caring professionals who minister to his / her medical needs. Give them hope and compassion in their care. And if it be your will, we ask for healing and a cure for _____.

Grant him / her ultimate freedom from his / her pain and suffering. All this we ask in the name of your son, who suffered for our sins. Amen.

Captain of Vessel

Our Lord and Savior Jesus, who calmed the seas with one wave of your hand, we request your blessing on Captain _____.

We ask that you would give him safe passage and calm seas. May his navigation be true and swift. May his crew be well trained and dedicated to their work. And may his passengers be safe and healthy during this voyage. Throughout the journey, give the ship a steady compass and a firm rudder. In Jesus' name we pray. Amen.

Caregiver

Gracious God, who cares for all of us, give your servant, ____ _____, strength and comfort as he / she cares for _____ We sometimes forget that the caregiver of the patient needs our prayers just as much as the patient does. And so we do ask that your comforting hands be placed upon _____ to soothe and protect him / her from depression or exhaustion. Your son, Jesus, healed many people during His earthly ministry, but He still needed time to be alone to renew His spirit. We ask that you renew the spirit of _____, and that you would grant him / her peaceful rest from his / her duties. We ask this in Jesus' name. Amen.

Ceasefire

Lord God, Father of the Prince of Peace, we ask that you would be with your children as this ceasefire goes into effect. Grant patience and resolve on both sides of the line. Help us to resist the temptation to reengage the conflict. Most of all, give us peaceful hearts and a quiet night. In Your name we pray. Amen.

Celibacy

Our Lord Jesus, who was blameless and without sin, the spotless Lamb of God, we ask that you would give our sons and daughters the strength and freedom to stay true to your commandments. Let their purity of heart and bodies serve as an inspiration to others who seek your holiness and truth. Help them to stand firm in their resolve to stay spotless and pure for you, O Lord. We thank you for their continued strength and dedication. In Jesus' name we pray. Amen.

Character

Heavenly Father, you well know the importance of character in a person. You realize that virtue and honesty are ideals that should be present in all of our lives. We pray that you would instill within us that same realization. We ask that you would help us to remember the utmost importance of character in a person.

We seek your help in striving to improve our own character. We know that we are sinful, but we also know that sin is a choice. To overcome such sin, we understand that all we have to do is ask for your strength through times of weakness. Help us to make choices that glorify you and your word. In your son Jesus' name we pray. Amen.

Charitable Cause

Giver of all things that are good, we pray for the ministry of _____. We ask for your guidance as you lead this agency in helping the downtrodden and outcasts of society. Give them the needed funds to continue their work within the community. Grant all who work for this cause a new sense of duty and dedication. Bequeath them strength in times of great need and suffering. Bestow patience upon them as they deal with the physical needs of your children. Help them to feed the hungry, to clothe the naked and to give shelter to the homeless. It is thankless work, but we thank you for their presence and selflessness. All this, we ask in your name. Amen.

Children

Lord God, we thank and praise you for your children. We express our deepest gratitude to you for their energy and enthusiasm toward life. We ask that you would keep them safe from harm and poor health. We thank you for their parents who gave them life. We would also ask that you give children a sense of obedience and honor as they grow in life. Help children to know that you really do love them, that you really do protect them and that you really do forgive them for their sins. We ask these things in your loving son's name. Amen.

Christmas Eve

Dear Lord, on that starry, starry night long ago, your son, Jesus, was born into poverty and humility. Tonight we come together to pay tribute to His holy birth.

We are so thankful for the gift of your son who brought the gift of eternal life to your children. Be with us now as we once again celebrate that wondrous night in Bethlehem. In God's holy name we pray. Amen.

Christmas Day

Our Lord Jesus, we celebrate your holy birth and welcome this new day of hope and wonder. Your birth has given us a new beginning, one that is free of sin and death. We know your humble nativity was needed to fulfill the prophecies, and we thank you for the ultimate sacrifice you made for us on the cross. Your suffering and death give us new life and renewed hope. Thank you again for your special birth and sacrifice. In your name we pray. Amen.

Christianity

Our Gracious Heavenly Father, we praise and thank you for your church and the people, your children, who are your church.

We come from many faiths and traditions, but we realize there is only one true God, and one true Messiah. Be with your church as it seeks out your will. Strengthen its people, as its ministers to your children. Renew their faith as they share the glorious Good News with others. In your son's name we pray. Amen.

Church

Lord God, your church marches on in faith and obedience to your will. We thank you and praise you for leading your children down the path of righteousness and virtue. Although we are all sinners, we know we have been forgiven by the blood of your son, Jesus Christ. As your church, continue to lead us; continue to strengthen us; continue to bless us in your holy ministry. Lead on O king eternal. In Jesus' name we pray. Amen.

Commanding Officer

Our Father and leader, be with our commanding officer as he makes the critical decisions that affect all of us. Give him strength and wisdom as he guides us in our military training. Mold us into

obedient soldiers. And if we are sent into battle, help us to do our duty no matter what the consequences. Help us to follow _____
_____with a firm resolve and to give all that we have in service to both our country and our commander. We pray this in the name of our Great Commander in heaven. Amen.

Community

Our Savior, we ask that you would give us a greater sense of community so that we might truly love our neighbors as ourselves. We come from many different backgrounds, ethnicities and traditions, but we are truly one people who only live to serve you and your children. Help us to do your will and to aid others who are in need. Put our hands to good use: to clothe the naked, to feed the hungry and to shelter the homeless. In your name we pray. Amen.

Complacency

Gracious Father, Giver of all that is good, grant that your children will not grow complacent to the wants and needs of others. You have blessed us abundantly, and we do not lack for anything. Help us not to forget those who may not be so richly blessed. Instill within us the desire to share what we have with others who are less fortunate than we. Help us to be active in support of your work and ministry here on earth. In your name we pray. Amen.

Confirmation

Lord Jesus, we pray that you would be with these sons and daughters who are confirming their faith today. They have dutifully studied your word for many months to bring them to this moment of confirmation. As they enter into you loyal flock today, give their faith a renewed strength. Bless their lives with a renewed purpose. Bestow their hearts with a renewed love for you and your children.

And as they live here today, freshly confirmed in their faith, give them a firm resolve not only to do your will, but also to share your word of hope with others. All these things we ask in the name of you, Our Lord and Savior. Amen.

Confession

Father God, we confess to you that we are weak and sinful beings. We ask for your mercy and pardon of our digressions. Forgive our unbelief, and strengthen us in times of trial and temptation. Give us a firm resolve to obey you and your commandments. Help us to resist the devil's trickery and enticements. And as we confess our failings, help us to remember that your son, Jesus Christ, suffered and died for us so that we would be made clean and whole again. We confess these things in the name of your son, the suffering servant. Amen.

Conservation

God, Creator of all things, you have given man dominion over all the earth's flora and fauna. Grant that we may be good stewards of your earthly kingdom. Help to use your resources wisely and sparingly. And give us the common sense to recycle material that can be reused to serve mankind. We simply ask that you would help us protect and preserve our environment in the manner in which you intended it. In our creator's name we pray. Amen.

Covenant

Father God, as the waters receded over all the land, and Noah and his family left the boat to once again inhabit the earth, you vowed to never destroy the earth with flooding again. And as a symbol of that promise, you sent a rainbow to seal that covenant. Help us, in return, to give you a promise as well—a promise that we will always obey you, love you and serve you. In Jesus, your son's name we pray. Amen.

Crisis

Lord, today as we stand at the crossroads of life-changing decisions, we pray that this crisis situation will mold us into better people. Give us the courage to act decisively and compassionately. Help us to do your will. Give us strength and the patience to see this crisis through to its fruition. And provide us with the wisdom to use this crisis as a teacher. Allow this experience to serve as a lesson to all of us, that you are a loving Father, and that you will protect and preserve your people today, tomorrow and always. Amen.

Cross-of Jesus

Dear God, we behold the cross of Jesus, your beloved son. On that tree your son selflessly gave His life for the forgiveness of our sins. As a result of His excruciating ordeal, we were washed anew. We thank you for making that sacrifice for us. We know how much he suffered—the shame he endured, the agony he felt—but we cannot begin to say how much that act of love and sacrifice has meant to us.

Our deep gratitude for our salvation from sin and our appreciation for eternal life are symbolized by the tears of Jesus, which bring living waters of everlasting life. We thank you and praise your name. Amen.

<u>Cruise</u>

Heavenly Savior who walked on water and calmed the raging seas, we ask that you would be with us on this voyage. Provide our captain with a steady compass as he pilots us on this journey. Grant the crew good health and a journey free from injury. Give this vessel a sharp keel as it cuts through the ocean's depths. All these things we ask in your name. Amen.

<u>Death</u>

Lord God, we have all experienced death, be it a relative or a close friend. During this dark hour, we search for answers to our questions of why. We seek you out to understand the meaning and purpose of this loss. We question our faith because we agonize over why you would take him / her from us. Help us to realize that death is a natural part of life. Help us to understand that you sent your son so we could all overcome sin and death. We humbly ask that you would welcome _____ into your kingdom. We know now that his / her pain and suffering is now gone, and that peace, love and serenity are now his / hers. We ask these things in your heavenly name. Amen.

<u>Disease</u>

Our Great Healer of the Ages, we ask that you would ease the pain of those suffering from disease. Mercifully hear their cries for an end to their agony. Grant them your healing touch and if it be your will, restore them to our fellowship.

Give them the freedom of good health and happiness so that they might once again actively fulfill your will. We ask this in your name. Amen.

Deliverance

Our Compassionate Father, we ask that you would give us deliverance over sin and death. Forgive our trespasses, and cleanse us of all our evil thoughts and actions. We live in a world that gives us many choices and options to live outside of your kingdom. The sins of the flesh entice us to go down wrongful paths. Our senses are bombarded with the smells, the sights and the sounds of digression. Lust and jealousy invade our very being to the core. Help us to keep our hearts open to you and your righteousness. Deliver us from the painful aftermath of lives gone astray. Strengthen our resolve to seek your love and forgiveness. In your holy name we pray. Amen.

Depression

Lord God, Giver of all that is good, we pray for _____ _, who is suffering from the agony of depression. Grant him / her a wise physician who knows that depression is treatable with the proper medication. Help others to recognize that this disease is not contagious, and that what _____ really needs during this trial is companionship and understanding. Give him / her serenity in life, and allow him / her to experience joy once again. In Jesus' name we pray. Amen.

Dinner Grace

Our Great Provider, who gives us everything we need, we thank you for the bounty of food that is before us. We thank you for the skillful hands that have prepared it. We ask that you would bless this food to our bodies that it might nourish us. May it strengthen and preserve us throughout this day. In God's name we pray. Amen.

Direction

Father, sometimes we go through life like a rudderless ship, zigzagging through the snares and troubles of life. We ask that you give us a firm and true course with your beacon of holy light. Allow us to follow your steadfast path. Let our eyes be transfixed on the compass of your love. Steer us into a steady wind of grace and forgiveness. In our Holy Captain's name we pray. Amen.

Discerning Gifts of the Holy Spirit

Almighty and Everlasting God, we pray for your Holy Spirit and the gifts that are bestowed upon us—the gift of teaching, the gift of preaching, the gift of speaking in tongues, the gift of compassion and healing. All these gifts come from you, and we ask that you would help us recognize these gifts. We request your guidance in using them for your glory, and the glory of your people.

Help us in our discernment of these gifts and strengthen us to use them in our daily walk with you. Give us the power and understanding to use these gifts with all wisdom and compassion. In your son's name we pray. Amen.

Discouragement

Lord, there are days when the whole world seems to crash down upon us. We experience sickness and death in the family. We receive unexpected bills, or we lose the trust and love of a life partner. Sickness may strike us, and we may lose a promotion or even employment. We understand that life is hard but help us to realize that you are always beside us, through the bad times as well as the good. Strengthen us when the road we travel becomes filled with obstacles and roadblocks. Always be with us to encourage and redeem us. In Jesus' name we pray. Amen.

Dishonesty

God, Giver of all that is good and righteous, be with me this day. Forgive the lies and deceit that overshadow my life. Give me courage and strength to be honest and straightforward in all my relationships. You know the dark valley in which I travel when lies and deceit overwhelm my life. Lead me to your light of righteousness. And let that light of truth overcome my failings. In Jesus, the perfect lamb's name I pray. Amen.

Dispute

Lord, we know that you rest on the side of righteousness and glory, but sometimes there are two opposing forces that claim that position. While we honor and respect both sides of an argument, we ask that you give us a sense of understanding and compromise as we search for a middle ground of reason and action. As we deliberate, grant us patience and hope that an amicable solution will soon come to pass. In God's name we pray. Amen.

Diversity

God of all people of faith, your children are a mixture of race, religion, ethnicity and tradition. We come from many different backgrounds and neighborhoods. Today we honor that diversity we come together to worship you as one body, united in our love for you and your children. Instill within our hearts a full measure of faith, patience and understanding as we walk with you and each other. Grant us unity of purpose and common hope. In your holy name we pray. Amen.

Doctor or Surgeon

Our Great Physician, we thank you for the skilled hands of doctors and surgeons. We express gratitude to you for their training and experience, and we thank you for the nurses and the hospital personnel who support their efforts. Strengthen these medical professionals in the coming days and weeks ahead as they endeavor to heal the sick and repair the injured. Guide their hands as they ease the pain of others. In Jesus' name, who healed us all with His body and blood, we pray. Amen.

Doubt

Great God and Father, we humbly ask that you would erase our doubt and unbelief. Give us faith to move mountains in your name. Sometimes tragedy invades our lives and we question our faith. During such times, we may even question your very existence as we ask the question—why? Help us in our period of unbelief. Give us the wisdom to seek you out. Enable us to understand that our human frailties can cloud our faith and our understanding. Give us a clear path to your love. In your name we pray. Amen.

<u>Drought</u>

Father Creator, who brings life to every living thing, we come before you with dry fields and thirsty crops. We ask that you would bring cleansing and refreshing rain down upon your land and people. It has been so long since the clouds have opened up to bring living water to us. We humbly ask that you would hear our cries for rain and that you would bring comfort to those farmers who are suffering the most. All these things we ask in Jesus' name. Amen.

Easter Morning

Our Father and Redeemer, we give you thanks and praise for this glorious Easter morning. On this day, your son, Jesus Christ, overcame sin and death by rising from the dead, and walking among us until His miraculous ascension. We are grateful for the pain and suffering that your son endured for us. Help us always to be mindful of that sacrifice. Wash us anew once again and give us strength to live each day as your loving children. All these things we ask in the name of the One who saved us. Amen.

Ecumenical Service

God of all faiths and devotions, we come before you from many divergent faiths and traditions. Give us the realization that there is only one true God, who reigns over all of us. Thank you for the freedoms we enjoy as citizens of this great nation. We are grateful for the opportunity to worship together as one without fear of persecution or arrest. Today, as we gather together as one, we pray that you give us the strength to speak with one voice among many voices. As you guide us today, lead us down the road to faith and forgiveness. In your holy name we pray. Amen.

Election

Father God, our Creator, we pray for our country as we go to the polls en masse to elect the President of the United States and other important leaders in Congress. Give our voting population the strength and opportunity to go to the polls and cast their ballots. We thank you that we live in a free republic where the people rule with fair and committed representation.

When our forefathers formed our constitution, they did so with prayerful consideration, as a nation under God. Give us, the electorate, that same feeling of prayerful consideration as we choose our leaders today. This we ask in your name. Amen.

Emergency

Our Lord Jesus, who met every emergency with calm resolve, we ask for your presence as we deal with this urgent crisis. We pray for the strength that is needed to make difficult decisions. We humbly ask for patience as we wait for a resolution to this difficult situation.

And we pray that we might learn from this experience so that we are prepared and ready in case such an emergency should arise again. All these things we ask in your name. Amen.

Empowerment

Lord God, as we come before you in thanksgiving, give us the power and courage to do your will on this earth. Help us to share the good news with others. Help enable us to minister to the sick, the hungry, the homeless, and those wandering purposelessly or without direction. Strengthen our resolve as we fight temptation and sin. Keep us bold in the faith as we witness to our neighbors, and give our neighbors a patient ear as they hear our confession of faith. In your son Jesus' name we pray. Amen.

Encouragement

Father God, Creator of all that is good, give us the strength and encouragement to live one day at a time. Make us mindful of the knowledge that you do not give us more than 24 hours of problems. We may become discouraged at times, due the sheer enormity of our problems, but help us to remember that you are always with us, even unto the end of time. Walk with us, side by side, and sustain us through our tribulations with your love, forgiveness and strength. In Jesus' name we pray. Amen.

Energy

Father God, Source of all light and enlightenment, we pray that you would continue to bless us with enthusiasm for the work that lies ahead. Help us to feed off your endless mercy and energy. Give us strength to fight off the devil and his tempting ways. Revitalize us as we seek to make disciples of all nations. Be present in our work on earth as we minister to the needs of your children, and help our work to be important and meaningful in your sight. In Jesus' name we pray. Amen.

Engagement

Our Mighty God and Father in heaven, we thank you for the lives of _____ and _____.We ask that you would be with them as they prepare to make the ultimate commitment to each other. Keep them patient and strong as they travel down this road of engagement and promise.

Grant clarity of thinking as they make plans and commitments for their life together. As they prepare to embark on their life together, give them compassion for each other's feelings. And in all that they do, help them to keep their eyes focused on you and your endless love. In your mercy we pray. Amen.

Enlightenment

Lord Jesus, you are the true light of the world. You so brighten our lives with your glorious love and forgiveness. Shine your love down upon us and help us to walk in that beacon of purity and life. Illuminate your ever-presence to us.

Without you and your love, there is darkness and sin. So let our light shine before all who wish to receive it. In your light and your love, we pray. Amen.

Enthusiasm

Lord God, we thank you for the vitality of life that you offer us. Help us to exude that vitality and to be enthusiastic as we share your love with others. Grant us a joy and zest for life that only you can bring. Empower us with zeal and passion as we live each day for your glory. And move us to fervently pray and follow you all the days of our lives, through Jesus Christ, we pray. Amen.

Epidemic

Lord Jesus, Great Healer and Savior, we pray for the health and well being of our nation, which lies in the grip of a disease that seems unrelenting and leaves many weak and dying in its wake. We seek answers as to why you would bring this sickness upon us. We know that we are a sinful nation, but we ask that you would have mercy on us. We beseech that you would bring us deliverance from this wretched disease. As you healed the paralytic who was lowered from the rooftop, end our suffering too. Bring us to a time of comfort and rest. And grant us your peace. In your name we pray. Amen

Evangelism

Our Savior and Redeemer, you sent us out to baptize and make disciples of all nations. Give us the strength to take that great commission very seriously. Instill within our hearts the passion and fire that is needed to evangelize and bring your everlasting love to others. Help us to heal in your name and to bring comfort to your children who suffer from loneliness or disease. Give us the inner power to share your word with all who will listen. These things we ask in your name. Amen.

Exultation

Our Lord, Great Father Almighty, your name is highly exalted, and we worship you with every breath of our being. You are the alpha and omega, the beginning and the end. In you there are no limits or boundaries. Your love is unending; your power is everlasting.

We come before you with reverence and humility. We simply ask that you would be merciful to your children and to forgive their sinfulness. With great awe and reverence we ask this, in your almighty name. Amen.

<u>Faculty</u>

Lord, we pray for the faculty of this institution of higher learning. We pray that you would give them strength to mold your children's minds in this upcoming semester.

We lift them up to you so that you might bless them with wisdom, integrity and patience. Our teachers and professors work with a double-edged sword, as they deal with demanding administrators and challenging students. Give them the power to work effectively with each group, and strengthen them with good health as they daily prepare for their classes. In Jesus' name we pray. Amen.

<u>Faith</u>

Dear Lord, we remember the time when Simon Peter denied knowing you three times before the rooster crowed twice. We feel the pain and anguish that Simon Peter felt as his faith deserted him. Help us overcome our unbelief. Give us a faith that can move mountains and sustain us through our most trying days. Strengthen our resolve to once again follow your will and word. And give us compassion for others as we share your love to those with a listening ear. In God's holy name we pray. Amen.

Father's Day

O God, Our Heavenly Father, we thank you for the gift of fatherhood. We thank you for the fathers who have raised us in your love. We express gratitude to you for their commitments and devotion to their children. We praise you as they take their responsibilities of parenthood seriously. And we ask that you would give them strength as they sweat and toil to provide us with food, clothing and shelter. We thank you for their efforts and we ask that you would be with them, guiding and supporting them in all that they do. All these things we ask in your son's name. Amen.

Fellowship

Great God, Giver of all that is good, we thank you for the fellowship we enjoy as your children. We stand together, side by side, and praise you for the forgiveness and eternal life that your son Jesus has brought to each and every one of us. Through Jesus' death and resurrection, we have overcome sin and death. We thank you for the salvation that we all enjoy as your children. Through your son Jesus Christ's name we pray. Amen.

Festival of Passover

Gracious God and Deliverer of life and mercy, we thank you for this Passover celebration when we remember the time the angel of death passed over the Hebrew people and spared their first-born children. We give thanks for the bounteous meal that celebrates this important festival. Bless the loving hands that have prepared it. May this food strengthen our bodies and spirits so that we might better stand in service to you, most holy God. In your name we pray. Amen.

Flag

Dear God, Protector of us all, we thank you for the flag that waves in freedom over our land. We praise you and thank you for the men and women who have defended and fought for this symbol of freedom. We are especially grateful for those who have given their last full measure of devotion in defense of our nation. With your son Jesus as their model, we express gratitude for those who would lay down their lives for us. And as our flag flies bravely in all corners of the world, help us to be proud of our heritage. Assist us in being resolute in our commitment to break the bonds of slavery and tyranny, wherever it exists. We ask these things in your name. Amen.

Flood Victims

Our Father Creator, we ask your blessing on the victims of the recent raging flood in _____. We ask that you would comfort the homeless, heal the sick and injured and to instill in the victims feelings of hope and optimism. Help them to be patient and understanding toward the emergency workers who seek to give them comfort and compassion. Help them to salvage as much as they can from their flood-ravaged homes, and provide them with the food, clothing and shelter they need to get back on their feet again.

We pray simply that you would stand beside them in these difficult hours and days ahead. In Jesus' name we pray. Amen.

Food Bank

   Our Gracious Lord, Giver of all that is good and holy, we thank you for the food that is provided to families who cannot afford it. We pray for each food kitchen and food bank in our area that you would give them the necessary staples to provide each hungry family with the much-needed food for their mealtimes. We know you will provide for them; we are confident that you will give the food bank workers patience and compassion as they deal with your hungry and needy children. Strengthen them in their service to you and your blessed children. All these things we ask in the name of Jesus Christ. Amen.

Forgiveness

   Great and Gracious Lord, we humbly ask you for the forgiveness of our sins. We beseech that you would be patient with our humanity and character defects. We know that we all fall short of the glory of God, but we still ask for your strength to resist temptation when it arises. We also pray for your mercy and ask you to wipe us clean and make us whole again through the body and blood of our savior, Jesus Christ. As you forgive our sins, help us to also forgive the sins of others. Assist us in starting each day with a clean slate, not looking back at our past transgressions. Rather, enable us to look forward in service to you. In Jesus' name we pray. Amen.

Freedom

Gracious and Holy Father, we sometimes take for granted the freedom and liberty we all enjoy as citizens of this beloved land. We also sometimes forget the ultimate sacrifice that was given for the preservation of that freedom. We thank you for the men and women who have given their lives for the defense of our liberty. We also express gratitude to you for those who were wounded in battle. We whole-heartedly thank you for those men and women who served our nation in times of war and peace. We thank you for their selfless sacrifice as well. As we continue to defend freedom around the globe, give us a firm resolve to break the chains of tyranny and enslavement, both at home and abroad. In God's name we pray. Amen.

Friendship

King of kings, and Lord of lords, we thank you for the gift of friendship—for those men and women who stand resolutely beside us in times of trouble and despair. As one of your precious gifts, you give us friends to brighten our days, to share our worries and troubles and to lighten our burdens. As we willingly receive that gift of friendship, help us to freely give that same gift to others. Help us to be compassionate and caring in our relationships with our fellow human beings. As you had an inner circle of trusted friends and advisors, give us patience and understanding with our inner circle of friends. And please help us to be friends to the friendless—to share with them your forgiveness and love for them. In our savior's name we pray all these things. Amen.

<u>Fruits of the Spirit</u>

Our God in heaven, you appointed some to be prophets, some to be teachers, some to be preachers, some to be healers and some to speak in tongues. We recognize that each of us is blessed with different gifts and fruits of the spirit. Help us in our discernment of these fruits and strengthen us to use the talents to your glory and to the glory of mankind. Grant us the wisdom to use these talents with proper respect and reverence. And always be with us as we seek your power and glory. In your son's name we pray. Amen.

G

<u>Global Peace</u>

Our Gracious Father, we pray for peace and serenity throughout the world. War rears its ugly head in many corners of the globe, and the pain and suffering that results from it is agonizing to all of us.

We know that war brings death and destruction to the earth, but we also know that peace brings hope and healing from the wounds of battle. Grant us peace in the world, and may it begin in the hearts of us all. In the name of the Prince of Peace, we ask this. Amen.

<u>Goodness</u>

Lord God, in your psalm you have said that goodness and mercy shall follow me all the days of my life, and I thank you for the daily goodness you give to me. For the many blessings in my life, I also give you thanks. Please forgive the bad behavior that sometimes takes hold of my life. We are all sinful human beings, and I ask for your forgiveness and mercy of my transgressions. Help me to be a good citizen and a loving servant of your people. In Jesus' name I pray. Amen.

Goodwill

Almighty God and Father, Giver of all that is good and holy, we ask that you would give this sometimes cruel world a breath of forgiveness and compassion. As the birth of your son, Jesus, brought goodwill to the hearts of others, allow that same goodwill to rest in our minds and bodies so that we might better serve you and your children. Give us strength to heal our troubled minds and suffering hearts so that we might bring your goodwill and peace to others. In your name we pray. Amen.

Gossip

Lord God, you teach us in the Ten Commandments to not bear false witness to our neighbors. This means you wish us not to spread hurtful and damaging lies about others. Help us to spare our brothers' and sisters' feelings and to not gossip about them. Doing so is wrong simply because it does not bring glory to you. As such, we humbly ask for your forgiveness of such wrongdoing. In Jesus' name we pray. Amen.

Grace

Almighty God and Father, pour out upon us your grace and favor. You have indeed saved us from sin and death through the body and blood of your son, Jesus Christ. Help us to be mindful that the grace and mercy you give us is free. All you ask us to do is to believe and have faith, to which we humbly oblige you. And so with faithful hearts we pray, in the name of your son, Jesus Christ. Amen.

Gratitude

Eternal Father, we come to you with our hearts filled with gratitude and love for you. We thank you for all that you give to us—the clothes on our backs, the food on our tables, the roofs over our heads and the happiness we all enjoy. We are grateful for the suffering and death of your son, Jesus. Thank you for that supreme sacrifice of giving your son so that we might overcome sin and death. Through your son, Jesus, we pray. Amen.

Graveside Prayer

Father, we praise you as we remember the life of _____. Comfort those who are mourning his / her passing. Help us always to remember that our time on this earth is fleeting and to live each day in full service to you and your children. We now commit the body of _____ to this final resting place. Earth to earth, dust to dust, ashes to ashes, we commend his / her spirit to you with the full promise that you will return and take us back to our heavenly home to live with you forever. In Jesus' name we pray. Amen.

Guilt

Forgiving Father and Gracious God, we know you sent your son Jesus to die for our sins. And so, we humbly ask that you would forgive us our sins and remove the guilt that cripples and paralyzes our existence. Help us to accept your forgiveness and to move on with our lives in service to you and your children. Ease our minds by absolving us of our transgressions. In Christ's name we pray. Amen.

ℋ

Hardship

Loving God and Father, we pray for the family of _____.
Bless them with the necessities of life that we take for granted. Give
them food, shelter and clothing to nourish their bodies and warm
them from the harsh winter cold. Grant them good health to help see
them through these difficult times. Give us the strength and desire
to assist them in any way that we can. You bless us abundantly with
your love and favor. Help us to share your love with the _____
___ family, that we may better know your love through our service
to them. In your son's name we pray. Amen.

Health

Lord Jesus, you healed so many people while you ministered on
this earth. We ask that you would send that healing strength to our
brother / sister, _____. He / she is suffering so much. We
humbly beseech that you would ease that suffering. Comfort him /

her with your abiding love and your gentle touch. In Jesus' name we pray. Amen.

Heart

Almighty God and Father, we ask that you would give us compassionate hearts as we seek to help your children who suffer from the pain and anguish of disease and injury. Instill within our hearts the joy of service so that we might jubilantly evangelize your word. Help our labors to be fruitful and to be joyful in your sight. With thanks we offer these prayers in the name of your son Jesus. Amen.

Heritage

Lord, we thank you for our heritage and ancestry. We thank you for the lives of our forefathers who courageously traveled to America to forge a new life of religious freedom and liberty. They struggled mightily to feed their families and to provide them with adequate clothing and shelter. We owe them much gratitude for the sacrifices they made so that we might live in the God-founded nation. We thank you for blessing their efforts, and we ask that you would strengthen us to continue their legacy of faith, hard work and devotion. In Jesus' name we humbly pray. Amen.

Home

Lord Jesus, Our Faithful Friend and Savior, we thank you for the gift of shelter from freezing cold and rain. Help us to realize that a home is more than just wood and brick. Aid us in always remembering that a home is where we go to seek refuge from the storms that life brings to us. Remind us that it is a place where we protect and nurture our families. Call our attention to the fact that it is a place where we teach our children to love and worship you. Remind us too that it is a place where we rest from the struggles of everyday life. Bless our home and all those who dwell within it. In God's holy name we pray. Amen.

Homeless

Lord God and Provider, we pray for the homeless people in our own community and across the nation. Comfort them and help them find shelter from the cold and rain. Strengthen us so that we can do all we are able to help them find shelter. We remember that your son was forced to live in a stable for His first few hours of existence and we thank you for His sacrifice. Help us to share all that we can, and strengthen all those who live on the streets. Give them hope in you and your children. In humility we pray. Amen.

Hope

Almighty God and Father, through the death of your son Jesus Christ, we have hope in the resurrection and the life. Your son overcame sin and death by suffering and dying on the tree on Calvary's hill. We thank you for the sacrifice of your son on our behalf. We pray that the hope of everlasting life it wrought can be shared with others. Give us the strength and means to spread that hope and joy. In Jesus' name we pray. Amen.

Hospice

Lord, we are thankful for the men and women who work in the hospice programs in our area. We pray that you would spiritually strengthen them as they deal on a daily basis with the pain and suffering of death. Help them to be a comfort to the loved ones who wait for a peaceful ending. Thank you for the ministry of hospice. May it always be with us to help ease the passing of our loved ones. In Christ's name we pray. Amen.

Hospital

Almighty Jesus, healer of the sick, and injured, we praise you and thank you for this medical facility. Stand steadfastly beside the doctors, nurses and medical staff members as they treat your children for various diseases and injuries. Strengthen the support staff members who work in the laboratories, the cafeteria, the laundry room and the maintenance and administration departments. Grant them the assurance that their work is pleasing in your sight. Through your name we pray. Amen.

Humanity

God, Our Maker and Redeemer, we pray for the humanity of our nation and world. Give us an attitude of caring and compassion for our fellow men and women. May our hearts be filled with your love and understanding. May our hands be outstretched as we reach out to others less fortunate. Strengthen us to help others in need of food, clothing and shelter. Help us to be forgiving of each other, just as you have forgiven us of our sins and failings. These things we ask in the name of your blessed son Jesus. Amen.

<u>Husband</u>

God, Our Creator, you made man in your own image. And you formed woman so that man would not be alone. Through the ages you have blessed the man-woman relationship with love and understanding. Today, we ask your continued blessings on the union of _____ and _____. We especially pray for (<u>husband</u>) as he works to support his new family. Give him the strength to meet the challenges of everyday living with which he will be faced. Provide him with a compassionate heart as he shares his life with (<u>wife</u>). Bless their union with love and faith in you. Through your son's name we pray. Amen.

I

Illness

Our Heavenly Father, we humbly ask for your healing touch. Illness is an unwelcome invader in the lives of those who are suffering. Comfort those who are afflicted by it, and give strength to those who are ministering to the sick—the doctors, nurses and pastors—who daily tend to the needs of those who are weakened by illness. Thank you for their tireless ministry of healing. In Jesus' name we pray. Amen.

Illiteracy

Almighty Father, we pray for your children who are challenged by words on the printed page. We ask that you would send them understanding and that you would equip them with compassionate teachers who can help them improve their literacy skills.

Your word is such a powerful instrument. Give your children the power to read it with clarity and comprehension. In Jesus' powerful name we pray. Amen.

Impatience

Lord, we pray for patience as we deal with the challenges of living in service to you and your children. Our loved ones sometimes disappoint us with their rash words and impulsive actions. Give us the patience to forgive them, as you have forgiven all of us. You know our every need, so we ask of you, Lord, that you would give us patience to wait for you as you take care of our every necessity. We wait patiently as we pray in your name. Amen.

Influenza

Almighty Father and Lord, we ask for deliverance from this epidemic of influenza. Please strengthen the people who are afflicted with this illness at this very moment. Place your healing hand upon them so that they might mend quickly. Give the doctors and nurses who are treating the sick your strength and compassion. In Jesus' name we pray. Amen.

Infant Death

Dearest Father in heaven, we ask that you would welcome our little angel, _____, into your kingdom. He / she briefly blessed us with his / her smile and presence and now we commend him / her back to you. We thank you for his / her life, and we pray for his / her parents that you would comfort them while they grieve over the loss of their little one. We do not ask why; we simply know that you love us, and that you will take care of _____ until we see him / her again in heaven. Please welcome _____ into your loving arms. Amen.

Insight

Lord God, Father, and Creator of the universe, you are a bright, shining beacon in the darkness of this world. We ask for your insight into and understanding of this sinful world that is so full of confusion and ignorance. Teach us to walk down your right pathways. Give us direction and purpose in everything that we do. And bring to us a greater meaning of why you have put us here on this earth. In your son's name we pray. Amen.

Intelligence

Lord, we pray for the intelligence and understanding of your children. We have so many questions that we want to ask you. We know so little about your awesome power. We are dwarfed by your intellect and amazed at the grandeur of your creation. Give us fertile minds that you might fill them with your holy word. Help our minds to be vital instruments of your will on this earth. Assist us in using our intelligence to serve you and your children. In Jesus Christ's name we pray. Amen.

J

Jesus (A Child's Prayer)

Dear Jesus, we thank you for our parents and for the loving care they have shown. We pray that you would help them to take care of us always. We ask that you would keep them safe from harm. We pray for our teachers. We pray that you would help them to be good teachers. And we pray that you would help us to be good students. In Jesus' name we pray. Amen.

Job

Blessed Savior, we ask that you would help _____ find employment in this very tight job market. Help him / her to be accepting of any position that will raise his / her self-esteem and aid his / her financial situation. Help us always to remember that all work is glorious in your sight. In Christ's name we pray. Amen.

<u>Joy</u>

Gracious Father in heaven, we thank you for the joy that you bring into our lives. You sent your son, Jesus, to earth to overcome sin and death. We thank you for that sacrifice and express gratitude for the joy that salvation brings to all of us. And we pray that you would strengthen us and encourage us so that we might bring that joy of salvation to others. In your son's name we pray. Amen.

<u>Justice</u>

Heavenly King, we know that human injustice is the result of human failure, frailty and original sin. Help us to know that justice will only live in the hearts of those who seek and hear your holy word. Strengthen your children in the fight for justice and equality for all. Grant us your favor as we seek peace, compassion and understanding on an earth that is ravaged by violence, hatred and injustice. Help us to see that there is a righteous light at the end of the unjust tunnel. In God's holy name, we pray. Amen.

Kindness

Lord, we thank you for your loving kindness. We express gratitude toward you for the love and forgiveness you have shown us in the body and blood of your son, Jesus Christ. Help us as your children to show that love to others. In Jesus' name we pray. Amen.

Kingdom of God

Our Gracious Heavenly Father, when your son Jesus was on this earth, he told his beloved disciple: "The kingdom is God is within you."

So why do we search, Lord, for your kingdom in heaven when you have already revealed its location to us? Help us to realize that your kingdom is within us, as a living symbol of your forgiveness and love. Encourage us to spread the light of your kingdom to others who live in fear and darkness. In Jesus' name we pray. Amen.

Kinship

Lord of lords, King of kings, we come together as one to celebrate our kinship with one another. Your body and blood has brought us together in fellowship and we celebrate our like-mindedness. We ask that you would use this body of believers who have gathered here today to spread the good news of love, peace and forgiveness. In your name we pray. Amen.

Knowledge

Our Father, Giver of all that is good and holy, we humbly ask that you would strengthen us to continue to seek your knowledge and will for us. You have blessed us abundantly with your holy word, and we thank you for sending your son to earth to fulfill the prophecy of that word. We know that knowledge is power, so encourage us to use that power to serve you and your children. In your mighty name we pray. Amen.

𝕷

Labor

Lord God, our Creator and Redeemer, we pray that our labor would be a pleasure in your sight. We work to put food on our tables, to protect our families with shelter and to clothe our loved ones. We humbly ask that you would help us and encourage us to use our labor for the betterment of others less fortunate than we. We sometimes take for granted all the blessings that result from our labor. So, we request that you help us always to be grateful and appreciative of that work which continues to enrich not only our own lives but the lives of others. Through your son, Jesus Christ, we pray. Amen.

Leadership

Our Sovereign Lord, we pray for the leadership of our nation. We pray for the members of Congress that you would grant them a single mindset of service to the citizens of our great nation. We pray that you would strengthen our president as he leads and serves our country. Give him the necessary courage to make the tough decisions that affect all of us. We also ask that you would continue to bless the members of his administration. Encourage them to use their power to be faithful servants rather than maniacal tyrants. And finally, we ask that you would be with our leaders in state and local governments. Empower them with a sense of purpose and meaning, as they serve your children. In the name of your son, Jesus, we pray. Amen.

Life

Father and Creator, we thank you for the life of your son, Jesus Christ. We thank you for his supreme sacrifice so that we may live in eternity with you. Forgiveness of our sins and attainment of eternal life are such precious gifts that sometimes we take them for granted. Help us always to live in the light of your joy and serenity. All these things we ask in the name of Jesus. Amen.

Light

Precious Savior, you are the light of the world. You came to this earth during a time of great sin and darkness. The earth had no hope of forgiveness or eternal life until you graced us with your presence. You came to die for us and to overcome sin and death with your resurrection. The darkness of sin has now been lifted with the light of your love. Help us to live daily in that light, to bask in its gloriousness and to spread its illumination to others. In your holy light we pray. Amen.

Loss of Loved One

Gracious Heavenly Father, we gather together to mourn the loss of _____. We will miss him / her terribly, but we celebrate his / her life on this earth. We pay tribute to how his / her worldly presence touched us. We ask that you would welcome _____ into your kingdom. Take good care of him / her until we will see him / her again in heaven. In Jesus' name we pray. Amen.

Love

Loving Father, we thank you for the love you have shown us in the life and death of your son, Jesus Christ. And when Jesus arose from the dead, our eternal life with you was verified. Sin and death were vanquished by your love and the sacrifice of your son. Be with us now as we walk this earth, sharing your love and forgiveness with all those who will listen. Strengthen our resolve to do your will and to serve your people. In the name of Jesus, who died for us, we pray. Amen.

<u>Mankind</u>

Father, Creator of all that is good and holy, we pray for all of your children on this earth. Our world is torn by disease, war and slavery. We seek freedom for those who are imprisoned by religious and tyrannical persecution. We seek relief for those who are ravaged by illness and injury. We ask serenity for those who plan and implement acts of terrorism.

We also ask for your healing touch for those victims of such senseless violence. Comfort those who mourn their dying loved ones.

We pray for the future of mankind that somehow each man and woman on this earth would seek peace and forgiveness through you, Our Ultimate Redeemer. In your son's name, we pray. Amen.

Marriage

Father, we pray for the marriage of _____ and _____
_____. Give them the strength to be patient and understanding with
one another as you proclaimed love should be. Help them to forgive
one another so that their lives might always be free of resentment.
Help them to trust one another and draw upon each other's strength
during times of need. We ask that you would give them loving hearts
that are eternally filled with your love, hope and forgiveness. Be
with them as they walk with you and with each other. In your love
we pray. Amen.

Meeting

Lord we ask your blessing upon this meeting of _____
_____. Be with us as we discuss issues and concerns that
affect all of us. Help us to listen carefully to each topic and potential
problem so that we might effectively address it. Give us compassion
and understanding as we wrestle with the important questions that
concern this organizational body. In your name, we pray. Amen.

Mercy

Merciful God and Father, we ask for your love and forgiveness.
All of us are sinful beings and we fall short of your glory every single
day. But through the body and blood of your son, Jesus, we are made
clean again. The light of your salvation destroys the darkness of
sin. Help us to freely receive that mercy and to selflessly give it to
others who have sinned against us. In God's merciful name we pray.
Amen.

Mighty

Dear God, mighty is your name and word. Your awesome power brings release to those who are enslaved by the darkness of sin. Your everlasting love brings peace and forgiveness to those who kneel before you in prayer. Raise your loving arms and bless your children, and help them to be a blessing to others in return. In your omnipotent name we pray. Amen.

Mother's Day

Dearest Heavenly Father, we thank you and praise you for the blessings of motherhood. We express gratitude to you for the care and understanding they extend to us. We ask that you would continue to bless them as they continue to bless us. Help them to realize that motherhood is both a challenging and a richly rewarding vocation and experience. For all that they do for us, we give you thanks. And help us to show our appreciation for them, not just on Mother's Day, but every single day. In Jesus' holy name we pray. Amen.

Mourning

Lord God, we mourn the loss of _____. We gather together today as one body to share our thoughts and memories of our friend and loved one. We celebrate his / her life, and we thank you for blessing us with his / her presence in our lives. As we commend his / her spirit to you today, we ask that you would welcome him / her into your kingdom. In your son's name we pray. Amen.

N

Nativity

Father of Our Lord and Savior, we thank you for the humble birth of your son, Jesus Christ. He was born into poverty and laid in a lowly manger for there was no room for Him in the inn. As we remember that starry night of the nativity long ago, help us to make room in our hearts for that little babe born in Bethlehem. In baby Jesus' name we pray. Amen.

Neighbor

Lord Jesus, you taught us in the parable of the Good Samaritan that everyone is our neighbor. Striving to practice that lesson, we ask that you would strengthen us so that we might help our neighbor in any way we can. If he is hungry, help us to feed him. If he is homeless, help us to find him shelter. If he is naked, help us to clothe him. For when we do these things for the needy among us, we are also doing them onto you. Encourage us to be a good neighbor to all our brethren. In your name we pray. Amen.

<u>New Year</u>

Father God, Creator of all, we thank you for bringing us safely to the dawn of another year. As we turn the page to a new calendar, help us to forgive ourselves for the sins of the past year. Help us to go forward now into this New Year with our hearts full of your glorious love and forgiveness. Encourage us to live each day suffused with your power and might so that the way of righteousness and obedience might be evident to us. Embolden us to seek your favor—and your wisdom. Help us to share our faith with others, and in this New Year, we humbly ask for your grace and love. In your gracious name we pray. Amen.

<u>Nurses</u>

Our Lord Jesus, Comforter and Healer of the sick and injured, we thank you for the ministry of healing provided by the nurses in our community. We thank you for the hands that soothe and comfort your children during their hours of sickness. We thank you for the compassion and concern that nurses bring to their profession. Strengthen them daily as they selflessly care for their patients. In your name we pray. Amen.

O

Operation

O God, we ask that you would be with _____ as she
/ he faces surgery on this day. Comfort her / his family as they
anxiously await the operation's results. Be with the doctors, nurses
and surgical staff as they prepare for and perform their important
lifesaving work. Finally, we ask that you would restore _____
_____ to our fellowship soon so that he / she might once again be
an active participant. We miss her / his presence so much. We ask
this in the name of Jesus, who healed the sick and comforted the
mourning. Amen.

Ordeal

Father in heaven, we pray that this ordeal of suffering might
soon be over. We know that you only give us 24 hours of trouble and
misery. And we pray that somehow you would ease this suffering
and restore us to a more normal way of life and existence. May this

pain and anguish be vanquished by the love and forgiveness of your only son, Jesus Christ. We ask this in your son's name. Amen.

Ordination

Lord, we humbly pray for your servant, _____, who is being ordained into the service of you and your church today. Be with him / her as he / she begins this new spiritual journey. Strengthen his / her faith, so that he / she might spiritually advance. Encourage him / her to continually study your word and to seek out your will in his / her life. Through your son, we ask this. Amen.

Pain

O God, Our Healer and Redeemer, we ask that you would ease the suffering and pain of your children who gather in fellowship this day. They are hurting physically, emotionally, mentally and spiritually. And so we ask that you would grant them release from the heartache of their pain and misery. Comfort them through all their strife and restore them to a richer life filled with health and happiness. We pray these things in the name of your son, Jesus Christ. Amen.

Pastor

Jesus, Good Shepherd, to all of your sheep, we pray for our shepherd, Pastor _____. You have blessed him / her with so many gifts that are used in your service. We thank you for his / her commitment to your children, and we ask that you would strengthen Pastor _____ as he / she continues to journey in the light of your love. In Your name, we pray. Amen.

Patience

Lord God, your servant Job was dealt so many setbacks in his life—so many that we could not possibly count them all. But still throughout it all, Job remained your loyal and loving servant. We thank you and praise you for Job's patience and resiliency; he is truly a model of steadiness for us. We would ask for that same patience and resiliency he exhibited in our own lives, especially when life deals us heavy blows of sorrow and disappointment. Keep us ever faithful to the one who calls us His own. Amen.

Peace

Lord Jesus, Prince of Peace, we humbly ask for a swift end to the conflicts that currently plague our nations. To know your peace, we must first ask for your forgiveness and understanding. If tranquility is to make a home in our countries, it must first make a home in our hearts. Grant us that feeling of internal peace, solitude and forgiveness, giving it to us by your body and blood, so that it might infiltrate the world. In your name we pray. Amen.

Penitence

Our Father, in heaven, we bow down before you in awe and reverence. We humbly ask for the forgiveness of our sins. We pray that you would take our iniquities and wash them clean through your son's body and blood. Through the goodness of your son, you have erased our failures and shortcomings and washed us anew. We are grateful for another chance to serve you and your children. Thank you for that fresh start forgiveness brings. In your son's name we pray. Amen.

Pet

Lord, we pray for our friend and family member, _____ __. We thank you for all of the years that he / she brought joy and affection to everyone in our home. He / she was our good and faithful servant to the end, an ever-present reminder of how we should serve you. We would ask that you would bless him / her and comfort him / her always. Amen.

Poor

Father God, who richly blesses our lives on a daily basis, we ask that you would bless the poor in our community. Grant us the ability to help them in any way that we can.

If they are hungry, help us to feed them. If they are lonely, help us to visit them. If they are homeless, help us to find them shelter. And if they are shivering in the cold, help us to locate coats and proper clothing so that they might endure the bitterly cold weather. Your son was born in a lowly stable, so he knows firsthand the needs of the poor in our community. We ask this in Jesus' name. Amen.

Power

Lord, we are humbled by your power and glory. Help us to harness that power of mercy and forgiveness as we share your good news of love and salvation with others. Help us to use your power in service to our neighbors. Assist us by always guiding us as we journey through life's winding and bumpy road. In God's powerful name we pray. Amen.

Praise

Beautiful Savior, we thank you and praise for your ultimate sacrifice for us. Our sins are washed away by your precious blood. We thank you for your suffering and dying on the cross so that we could one day live again with you in heaven. We raise our voices in song as we praise you and thank you for that ultimate sacrifice. In your name we pray. Amen.

Prayer

Father, we come before you on bended knee, asking for your love and forgiveness. We pray that you would be with us this day as we seek to do your will and to serve your children. We pray for our friends and neighbors who are still seeking answers to their questions of faith and mercy. Illuminate for them the truth. We pray this in your son's name. Amen.

Pregnancy

Father God, Creator of all things, we thank you for the gift of life that lives inside our sisters of the faith who are pregnant. Grant them good health and patience as they grow and nurture their children. And as birth draws near, grant them safe and healthy deliveries so that their offspring might robustly serve you. In Jesus' name we pray. Amen.

Pride

Dear Lord, we ask that you would deliver us from the sin of pride and self worship. It is written in your word that the first shall be the last, and the last shall be first. Help us and strengthen us to be humble in our dealings with others. Indeed, encourage us to serve others without thought of fame or earthly reward, for we know that a far greater reward awaits us in heaven. Make us ever mindful of your promise so that we might overcome our vanity and egotism. In Jesus' humble name we pray. Amen.

Procrastination

Dear God, Our Father in Heaven, we ask for your patience as we deal with the character defect of procrastination. Help us to rise each day with renewed vigor and purpose, as we seek to do your will. Strengthen us to complete tasks with swiftness, dedication and respect.

Let us not put off for tomorrow what we might accomplish today. Help our work to be worshipful and honorable in your sight. In your name we pray. Amen.

Providence

Our Father, we ask for your guidance as we go about the tasks of everyday living. Make our paths straight and narrow in service to you and your children. Give us a clear vision of your will for our lives. And grant that our purpose in life be faith based upon and dedicated to you and your children. In the name of your son, Jesus, we pray. Amen.

Quest

Creator God and Father of us all, we ask that you would bless this spiritual journey that we endeavor in your name. We daily search for your word's meaning in our lives, and we thank you for the opportunity to serve you during this most important voyage of faith. May every foot we travel be undertaken with your glory at the forefront. Be with us now and forever. Amen.

<u>Recovery</u>

Lord Jesus, we come before you with heavy hearts as we pray for the recovery of _____, who is injured and being treated in the hospital. Be with the doctors and nurses as they endeavor to heal his / her broken body. Comfort _____ as he / she recovers from his / her injuries, ease his / her suffering and grant him a swift and complete recovery. We pray this in the name of the Great Healer, Jesus Christ, Our Lord. Amen.

<u>Refuge</u>

Lord of lords and King of kings, we ask that you would grant refuge to the sick, the lonely, the hungry, the thirsty and the homeless. Give them the courage to seek out protection and forgiveness in your everlasting love and mercy. Grant them healing when they are sick and injured, living water when they are thirsty, the bread of life when they are hungry, comfort when they are alone and shelter when they are homeless. We ask these things in your divine grace and wisdom. Amen.

Renewal

Father God, Creator of all that is good and righteous, we ask that you would bless our fellowship with renewal of your holy spirit. Strengthen our faith so that we might effectively share your good news with others. Grant us your divine wisdom as we seek ways to better serve you and your children. In Jesus' name we pray. Amen.

Responsibility

Our Gracious Heavenly Father, we ask that you would strengthen us so that we might be responsible children of your kingdom here on earth. Help us to be good stewards of your creation. Assist us in using your natural resources in a responsible way, conserving as much as possible for future generations so that they might also use and enjoy them. Help us to realize that the environment is ours to take care of. Empower us to perform that very important task in your holy name. Amen.

Rest

Father, Creator of the Universe, we know that you rested on the seventh day to order that you might enjoy your creation. And in the Ten Commandments, you require from us that we remember the Sabbath day to keep it holy. So on this Sunday, when we gather together to worship and praise you, encourage us to rest from our labor. Foster our enjoyment of your creation and natural wonders. Grant comfort and rest to those who are sick or grieving for a loved one. And when the sun rises tomorrow, help us to be refreshed and renewed for the coming week of work and service. These things we ask in your glorious name. Amen.

Resurrection

Lord Jesus, you are the resurrection and the life. Those who believe in you will live and never die. When we remember that empty tomb, we realize again that you arose from the dead and, in so doing, that you overcame sin and death. Thank you for suffering for us on the cross, for enduring the humiliation of crucifixion, for feeling the cruel nails in your hands and feet, for wearing the excruciating crown of thorns and for dying in such agony. On the third day, you lived again. You appeared before your disciples as tangible proof of the promise. Instruct us as you instructed them, to spread your good news of salvation and everlasting life with others. In your glorious name we pray. Amen.

S

Savior

Jesus Our Lord, we thank you for saving us from sin and death with your selfless sacrifice. You took the heavy burden of our sins and bore them on the cross on Calvary, not because you had to, but because you wanted to.

You loved us so much that you endured the excruciating nails, the agonizing crown of thorns, and the piercing of your side. And you did all of this solely so that we may be free from sin and death. Thank you for saving us with your resolve and precious blood. In your name, we humbly pray. Amen.

School

Dear God, we thank you for our school, which affords us a sound education. We praise you and thank you for the teachers and administrators who strive to make our school the very best it can be. Strengthen those who teach us so that they might continue to impart their wisdom. Encourage those administrators who have the responsibility of taking care of us. Keep us safe in our daily recess, and enrich us with your love as we learn those valuable lessons of life, each and every day. In your son Jesus' name we pray. Amen.

Serenity

Lord God, Heavenly Father, we know that inner serenity is such a fleeting and fragile feeling. In this world that is marred by hatred, violence, racism and intolerance, peace and tranquility are the most valuable and sought-after commodities. We fully realize that only you can give us that feeling of serenity and forgiveness through the body and blood of your son, Our Savior, Jesus Christ. Your son died so that we can live with you forever. That feeling of peace and hope should dwell within our hearts and should infuse us with an inner serenity that will last forever. In our Lord's name we pray. Amen.

Service

Dear Jesus, Our Lord and Savior, you came to this earth to serve mankind. And through your agonizing death—and subsequently—your glorious resurrection, you gave us newness of life and eternal salvation. Encourage and strengthen us to serve your children in the same generous manner—to be willing to risk our lives so that others may live. In your precious name we pray. Amen.

Service Men and Women

Lord God, please be with our fathers, our mothers, our daughters and our sons who are currently serving our country in the armed forces. Whether they are serving at home or deployed abroad, we humbly ask that you would keep them out of harm's way and that you would return them safely to their families. When they travel, grant them safe passage, and when they are in the heat of battle, give them the gentle assurance that you are always with them. In Jesus' holy name we pray. Amen.

Sickness

Father in Heaven, we ask that you would place your healing hand on _____. Give him / her strength to meet each day with a renewed commitment to fight this terrible disease that afflicts him / her.

Equip the doctors and nurses with compassion and patience as they endeavor to ease his / her pain and suffering. Most of all, Lord, we ask for _____'s deliverance from the anguish that he / she is enduring. Grant him / her a restful night of sleep, and the assurance that you are always with him / her. In your son's name we pray. Amen.

Sister

Lord God, I ask for your presence in the life of my sister, ___ _____. She is so lonely and disconsolate. She is so depressed by a life that has given her so much pain and heartache that she requires your assistance to go on. I simply ask that you would be with her during her hour of need. And help me to do all that I can to comfort and protect her from further suffering and anguish. Please reassure her that she is loved and cared for and give me the strength to console her today, and everyday. In Jesus' name I pray. Amen.

Sleep

Lord, you are the Prince of Peace, and I humbly ask that you would grant me the inner peace and serenity I need to have a good night's sleep. Many worries and troubles invade my thoughts each night. Help me to give those worries to you and to trust fully that you will take care of me. I know that you give me only 24 hours of trouble in a day, never more than that. As such, I ask you to help me live one day at a time, meeting the challenges of the new day with faith and resolve. I ask this in the name of the Prince of Peace. Amen.

Sobriety

Lord God, as I go to bed this evening, I thank you for giving me another day of sobriety. And as I wake up tomorrow, help me to face the morning with a renewed commitment to abstain from this harmful addiction. You continue to strengthen me as I walk down this road of recovery, and I thank you for that strength. Please help me to assist others, in some small way in finding the serenity that I have found in your love and forgiveness. In the name of the One who saved us all, Jesus Christ, I pray this. Amen.

Solitude

Dear God, we find peace in solitude. We know you are with us in the silence. We know you hear our breathing and that you listen to our soft and silent cries of praise and worship. In the darkness and tranquility, you speak to us in gentle tones of reassurance and love. We thank you and praise you for the opportunity to be alone with you and our thoughts. Through your serenity, we find peace and commitment. In your holy name we pray. Amen.

Sprit

Our Lord God, you sent your Holy Spirit to the apostles after Jesus ascended into heaven. It was then that your spirit gave them the gifts of preaching, teaching, speaking in tongues, healing and prophesying.

We know these gifts can only come from you, and we pray that as 21st century apostles you would again send your Holy Spirit to breathe on us. We ask that you would allow your Holy Spirit to infuse us with that same power and understanding. Encourage us to use those gifts of the Spirit to proclaim the good news that you have saved us from sin and death.

Let us make it known that through the suffering, death and resurrection of your son, Jesus Christ, you washed us anew. All this we pray in the name of the Father, and of the Son, and of the Holy Spirit. Amen.

Spring

Our God, you are an awesome God, full of power and majesty. You have blessed us again with this beautiful season of spring. The birds are singing their melodies once again. The trees are budding into verdant lushness once again. The flowers are preparing to bloom into full blossom once again. The sun is bright and warm once again. We remember that spring brings with it newness of life and a spiritual awakening for all of us. During this time of illumination, we ask that you would strengthen us to renew our commitment to serve you and your children. Through Christ, Our Lord, we pray. Amen.

Stress

Lord, we live in a hustle-bustle world that dominates our time and attention. We humbly ask that you would give us a moment of pause each day to rest and enjoy your beautiful creation. All too often, we take your world and its beauty for granted. We travel quickly through the day, never stopping to enjoy a glorious sunrise, the singing birds or the vibrant color of the green, green grass. Help us always to be grateful for your creation, and for the changing seasons. Let them serve as reminders to us that you love us always, from one glorious season to the next. We pray this in Jesus' name. Amen.

Success of Service Project

Father and Creator of all that is good, we ask your blessings upon our service project. In today's ladder-climbing society, we use the word "success" so flippantly that it is sometimes hard to define. We sometimes gauge the success of a service project solely by the amount of money we raise. We should realize, however, that success should really be measured by the number of people we help with the money we raise or the work we do. We sometimes ask, "What's in it for me?" Give us the mindset that service to others should be done without thought of personal gain or reward.

We should work for the welfare of others because we want to, not because we have to. Help us to see this as the true meaning of service. We thank you for this opportunity to serve, and we pray this in Jesus' name. Amen.

Suffering

Lord, we pray for our friend and neighbor, _____, who is suffering at this hour with a terminal disease. We ask that you would comfort him / her in these final days. Ease his / her pain and transition.

And when his / her anguish is finally over, welcome him / her into your loving arms to live with you in eternity.

Grant him / her a peaceful passing, and comfort those friends and relatives who remain behind on this earth. Give them the realization that they will one day join _____ in heaven to be with him / her forever. In Christ's name we pray. Amen.

Support

Our Heavenly Father, we ask for your love and support to get us through another day. We thank you for a restful sleep last night and we express gratitude for the glorious sunrise that greets us daily. Be with us now, through every minute of every hour, as we go about the daily tasks of living and working. Strengthen us to keep us free from harmful behavior. Help us to treat ourselves with love and respect and to treat others in that same light.

In your holy name we pray. Amen.

Talent

Lord of lords and King of kings, we thank you for the talents that you have given each of your children. Help us to use those talents to the glory of your holy name. Strengthen us to put those special gifts to use in your service and in the service of your children. Grant us the ability to grow and develop our talents, to their fullest potential so that their usage will become truly edifying to you. We ask this in your name. Amen.

Task

Lord God, as in any task, we ask for your power and direction. Help the fruits of our labor to be glorious in your sight. And though the task before us may appear to be daunting and challenging, enable us to accomplish it with joy and determination. May our labor be faithful in your eyes and cheerful in ours. In Jesus' name we pray. Amen.

Teachers

Our Father, we thank you for the faith and commitment our teachers exhibit. We ask that you would instill within their hearts complete joy and satisfaction for the work they are doing. In molding young minds and in setting a shining example of service to the children of our community, they are prime examples of your work. Give them wisdom, patience and understanding as they prepare their lessons for the day. Always be with them and strengthen them when their days prove long and challenging.

We thank you and praise you for their heartfelt instruction. In your son's name we pray. Amen.

Temper

Almighty King and Master, we thank you for the patience you have shown toward your children. We pray especially for your children who possess bad tempers and angry demeanors. We know that life can be frustrating, but that is no excuse for harming another human being. Please give those individuals control over their behavior. We also ask that you would grant them a more peaceful and serene existence. Show them the way to kindness, gentleness and love. In Jesus' name we pray. Amen.

Temptation

Dearest Jesus, for forty days you were tempted by the devil and all his fiendish ways. He offered you food when you had none. He proffered you the world, but you resisted. He told you to throw yourself off the temple pinnacle and have your guardian angels protect you from harm, but you did not listen to him. Give us that same faith and strength to resist his bait when we are tempted by the devil's charms. Help us to resist the temptation of sinful pleasure and satisfaction. In your strength we pray. Amen.

Thanksgiving

Lord God, Provider of all that is good and holy, we have set aside this day to thank you for the many blessings you have given us this year. We are so grateful for the health, happiness and love we all enjoy in your name. Help us to realize that we should give thanks not just today, on Thanksgiving Day, but every day and always because you have done so much for us. You sent your son, Jesus, to this earth to suffer and die for us so that we might overcome sin and death. For that we express our deepest gratitude. Again, we thank you and glory in your son's holy name. Amen.

Third World Countries

Our Father, you have blessed our country with abundance. As a nation, we are blessed to have food, shelter, adequate clothing and the best health care system in the world. But there are other nations, however, that struggle in their existence. They lack clean, safe drinking water. They are in need of more food because rains and floods have destroyed their crops. They lack shelter because earthquakes and other natural disasters have made them homeless. They suffer from disease as a result of a lack of adequate medical facilities, supplies and personnel. Thousands are dying daily from the ravages of AIDS, diphtheria and malaria. It is for those nations that we come to you in prayer. Won't you grant some relief to those poor countries? Strengthen those who have bountiful harvests so that they might share their grain with those who are hungry. Ease the third world inhabitants' suffering, and help us to do all that we can for them. In your son's name we pray. Amen.

Time

Father God, you grant us 24 hours everyday to make a difference in the lives of others. We are so grateful for that time, and we ask that you would help us to use it wisely. Bring us together to make time our friend instead of our enemy. The more believers we have for a project, the more time we have to minister to those children who are less fortunate than we are. Help us always to realize that time is fleeting and can never be recaptured.

As such, help us to make every minute count as we continue your ministry on earth. In your glory we pray these things. Amen.

Travel

Lord, during this busy season of travel, we ask that you would bless your children as they journey far and wide. Give them safe passage to their destinations, and grant them a peaceful and restful vacation so that they might return with a renewed purpose and vigor. Bring them safely home to us refreshed and reenergized so that they might more actively serve you and your children. In your name we pray. Amen.

Trust

Dearest Father, we know that trust is such a guarded and fragile emotion. Sometimes loved ones disappoint us and occasionally trust is fleeting, so we ask that you would help us to forgive and trust again. We know it is not easy to trust someone, especially when addictive behavior is repeated. We would simply ask for continued patience as that fractured trust is slowly rebuilt again brick by brick. Always, we pray this in Jesus' name. Amen.

𝒰

<u>Uncertainty</u>

Lord, we truly live in uncertain times. Violence and terrorism can strike in a split second. An auto accident can claim the life of a friend or loved one. Disease and old age can rob us of our independence before we even know it. A sudden economic downturn can negatively affect the way we live, both now and in the future. So many outside influences can effectively change us in the blink of an eye. We realize, however, that there is one certainty in our lives, and that is your love for us through the body and blood of your son, Our Lord and Savior Jesus Christ. Through Christ's suffering death we claim victory over sin and death. This is most certainly true. In Jesus' holy name we pray. Amen.

<u>Understanding</u>

Our Heavenly Father, we pray for understanding and discernment of the spiritual gifts that you have graciously given to each of us. Empower us to seek your will in our lives so that we might put those gifts to their utmost use. Some of us are teachers, preachers, singers, evangelists, administrators and healers and so we ask that you would strengthen us as we grow in the understanding of the spiritual gifts and talents with which have been bestowed. Help us to be faithful to your holy word in all that we do. In your son's precious name we pray. Amen.

Unity

Holy Father, grant us unity of faith and purpose as we proclaim your glorious good news to others. We fully realize that we are one body, called together in one faith and holy baptism. We are your children, bought with the precious body and blood of your son, Our Lord and Savior Jesus Christ. Under one faith, one Lord, one baptism in the unity of the Holy Spirit, we humbly ask that you would be with us always. In your mighty name we pray. Amen.

<u>Valor</u>

Our Lord and Savior Jesus Christ, we thank you for the valiant courage it took for you to suffer and die for our sins. Without hesitation, you allowed yourself to be nailed to the cross to bear our sins. Through your agony and death, we are made clean again. Our sins are washed away, so that one day we will live with you in eternity. Strengthen us to be bold and courageous in our faith. Grant us the conviction to take up the cross and follow you wherever that may lead. May our faith and witness be pleasing in your sight. In your name we pray. Amen.

<u>Vanity</u>

Gracious God and Father, we ask for the strength to resist the sin of vanity. We know that appearance is important, but we mustn't take it to the extreme of self-love and self-worship. Help us to set aside our arrogance and be humble in our service to others. Strengthen us also to live lives of devotion and service to you and your children. In your holy name we pray. Amen.

Victim of Crime

Lord we pray for our brother / sister, _____, who was severely wronged. Give him / her courage and strength to recover from this heinous crime. We don't understand why you allow such things to happen, but we do know that you love us. We find solace in the fact that you will ease such suffering and pain. We ask that you would be with the men and women who inflict injury and wrongfulness on others. Give them remorseful and repenting hearts so that they might seek out your love and forgiveness. In Jesus' name we pray. Amen.

Victory

Almighty God and Father, you sent your son Jesus to this earth to suffer and die for our sins. Through Jesus' precious body and blood, we now claim victory over sin and death. We now hold prize to eternal life. We thank you for the supreme sacrifice of your son. Help us to live lives of faith toward you and in service toward others as an outward expression of that gratitude. In Jesus' name we pray. Amen.

Virtue

Lord God, we ask for the strength to lead lives of virtue and devotion. Our bodies are temples of the Holy Spirit. As such, they should be treated with respect and honor. Deliver us from sins of the flesh and instant physical gratification so that we might extend to our bodies the respect that is due them. Our lives and bodies should be holy and precious in your sight.

Help us to be shining examples of purity to others. All this we ask in the name of your perfect son, Jesus Christ. Amen.

<u>Volunteers</u>

Gracious Lord and Savior, we thank you for our wonderful staff of volunteers. They selflessly give so much of their time and talents. It is heartening to know that there are people out there in the world who really care for others and are willing to serve you, without thought of payment or reward. Please strengthen them always so that they might continue to serve as examples to others. We ask too that you give others the same courage to step forward and help out in any way that they can. In your name we pray. Amen.

Weakness

Father, we know you are strong and powerful. We ask that your mighty hand would strengthen us in our day-to-day living so that we might overcome our failings. When the devil tempts us, he knows that we are at our weakest. So, give us your strength to resist the lure of Satan and his fiendish ways. Like your son who prayed in the Garden of Gethsemane, we ask for courage to face the challenges that lie ahead. In your strong son's name we pray. Amen.

Wonder

Creator God, we wonder at the glory of your creation. Each mountain, each valley, each river and each ocean has your master's stroke of grace and beauty indelibly stamped upon it. Help us to share that beauty with others. Help us also to never take your creation for granted, so that we might continually remain in awe of your splendor. We stand in reverence of your glorious and perfect

Bob Haar

creation. And we are grateful for everything that you do for us, your children. In your magnificent name we pray. Amen.

Work

Lord, we are grateful for the work that you have given our idle hands. We pray for the work that puts food on our table and a roof over our heads. We request also that our work would be always be pleasing in your eyes. And for those who are out of work and searching for a job, we ask that you would help them with their physical needs while they seek employment. Give them strength and persistence, and ultimately success, in securing gainful employment. In your name we pray. Amen.

Worship

Our Gracious Heavenly Father, we gather together today to worship your holy name. There are many different voices that are lifted up to you in song.

But despite our outward diversity, we are one in body and spirit. So too, we are unified in our praise for you. We humbly ask that our unified worship and praise are glorious in your sight. In your son's name we pray. Amen.

World Hunger

Our Lord God, Creator of all that is good and holy, we pray for the needs of those countries who have hungry children within their borders. It is so sad to see starving children. We ache so much for their neediness that we want to reach out to them and feed them ourselves. It is so hard to do that, but that is why we have Lutheran World Relief, Feed Your Neighbor and other hunger agencies to assist us. Help these charitable organizations in their very important work and strengthen us to personally do all that we can to help feed a child. In Jesus' name we pray. Amen.

Υ

<u>Youth</u>

Lord we pray for the youth in our congregation and in our community. It is so difficult to be young in this day and age. There are so many negative images and sinful choices available to our younger generation. Peer pressure does not help the situation. The temptation to opt for instant highs and physical gratification is so intense that we simply pray that our children would ask for your strength and power to resist the devil and his evil ways. We pray also that our young people would seek you out and gather together with other Christian teenagers to fight Satan's power and influence as a group. We humbly pray this in your name. Amen.

3

Zealousness

Father, we ask for zeal in our devotion to you and your word. We seek your will in our lives and ask for the power to carry out that will, whatever it may be. Strengthen our determination and solidify our resolve to serve you and your children. All power and glory are yours, now and forever. Amen.

If there is a prayer subject that you would like to see included in my next book of prayers and poetry, please e-mail me at bobh111099@msn.com Thank you.

About the Author

Bob Haar is currently the pastoral assistant at First St. John Lutheran Church in Toledo, Ohio. Mr. Haar has a Bachelor of Arts in Communication and English Literature from the University of Toledo, and earned a Master of Arts in Religion degree from Trinity Lutheran Seminary in Columbus, Ohio. He has been writing sermons for over 25 years, and is currently teaching catechism, preaching, designing worship services, leading bible studies, and visiting shut-ins.

Mr. Haar lives with his wife and two daughters in northwestern Ohio.

Printed in the United States
24926LVS00004B/172-189

9 781420 804096